USING PRINTED PAPERS

IN RAILWAY MODELLING

PETER SMITH

ISBN—13: 978-1505358476

ISBN —10: 1505358477

CONTENTS

CHAPTER 1

INTRODUCTION

Let me show you a picture.

When I built this LBSCR station building in 7mm scale during 2009, I was really proud of it. The prototype is a delight, and the model came out really well.

However, something was nagging at me; when I looked at the photographs, it looked like a model. No one was ever going to look at the picture above and be fooled into thinking they were looking at a real building.

The problem is with the walls and the roof. They are painted plastic, and they look like painted plastic. They don't look like bricks and clay tiles.

There had to be a better way.

There is...and that is what this book is all about.

Here's another picture.

This is also an LBSCR station building, modelled in 7mm scale.

Now, though, the bricks look like bricks and the clay tiles look like clay tiles, and the picture could convince someone that they are looking at an image of a real building.

The difference is in the way that the surfaces are covered, using printed papers instead of paint. In this picture the bricks, stone and tiles are paper, the tarmac is paper, the stained glass is paper and the posters are of course also paper.

Printed paper, a cheap, easy to use medium, has transformed this model into a convincing replica that looks realistic. I could never have achieved that with paint, so now I don't try. That first LBSC station building was the last model I finished entirely by painting. Now I know a better way, and once you have read this book, so will you.

CHAPTER 2

WHY USE PRINTED PAPER?

The use of paper in modelling had has a bad press. Older modellers remember embossed card rolling stock kits and building papers on which the image had been drawn or painted, which looking back on them were pretty awful. Roye England used to emboss bricks into sheets of paper when he built the cottages for Pendon and then paint them, one brick at a time.

Technology however has moved on, and the great leap that enables us to do so much more these days is that we can reproduce a photographic image, whether it's of a brick wall, a whole building or a 1930's poster. Now it is no longer necessary to produce a piece of artwork by drawing the image by hand as was done when Superquick kits were introduced in the 1960's. In the 21st century, the computer is just as necessary a part of the modellers toolbox as the scalpel and the steel rule.

Using a computer and simple easy to use software you can produce your own building papers, posters, etc. so that you get exactly what you want for your model. If you are happy to bypass that part of the process, though, and simply buy commercial papers, there is still a huge amount that you can do. Let's have a look at the advantages:

- Paper is cheap; a colour photocopy on A4 paper costs around 50p. At that price you can afford to experiment, and if you waste some it doesn't really matter.

- Paper is easy to use; it cuts easily, it can be stuck easily, it can be folded and curved.

- Paper is easy to store and has a long shelf life.

- There is no mess, no waiting for paint to dry, in fact instant results.

- You can print virtually anything on the surface, and then have multiple identical copies run off on a colour copier with ink that is colour fast and not affected by damp or sunlight.

- Using real photographs printed onto the paper you can reproduce surfaces that would be all but impossible to paint.

- Using paper you can create your own images for building papers, backscenes, etc. rather than ending up with something everyone else is also using.

- The image can be reproduced in any scale using the photocopier in your local print shop.

- If you make a mistake, just stick a new piece over the top.

These pictures should give you some idea of the possibilities.

This Settle and Carlisle station building in 7mm scale would have been very difficult to build without using paper. The random stone for the walls is paper, printed with an image of a real random stone wall. The dressed sandstone around the openings and on the corners is paper, which can be folded around corners, cut to shape easily, and has the pleasing variation in tone that would be very difficult to achieve by painting. It looks like stone because it is a photograph of real stone. The slates on the roof are paper; the sheet was just stick in place, there is no cutting into strips or even individual slates. Because it is a photo there are shadows, so it look three dimensional. The LMS poster boards are paper, printed with authentic 1930's posters. The ridge tiles are paper, a picture of real ridge tiles with real moss and lichen!

Look at the variation in the colours on the roof; could you paint that? I couldn't.

Don't run away with the idea that paper can only be used for walls and roofs though; here the net curtains are just printed on flat paper, but they look three dimensional and were a lot easier than modelling the full interior. Those checked table cloths are paper, as of course are all signs. This is in 1/32nd scale, so there techniques are of use even in the large scales. I have used them in every scale from 2mm up to gauge 3 and 16mm.

The layout below is 4mm scale, and here the papers are used for the platforms, the road surface, the stone wall, the edging stones and the cattle dock. No painting, no mess, no waiting for it to dry.

Like any modelling technique, printed papers aren't suitable for everything; you use them where they are appropriate and something else where they are not, just like with any other material or method. You'll be amazed how much you can do with them, though.

That gravel platform surface in the lower picture is printed paper—no mess!

CHAPTER 3

CREATING YOUR OWN PAPERS

If you are happy to purchase commercial papers ready to use you'll probably want to skip this chapter….I hope some of you do because I sell papers myself! However, if you fancy having a go at making your own here's how to do it.

Let's begin with a simple A4 sized sheet of brick, ready to be used on a building. I find A4 a convenient size to use, big enough for most walls but small enough to store easily.

You're going to need a digital camera and a computer, which I am sure most modellers already own and use. I use a Fuji Finepix camera which I simply set to Automatic and leave to get on with all the hard stuff itself—it works a treat. It has a Macro setting for photographing models too, very useful.

I like to use a PC for this work as the big screen is useful and I like using a mouse, but I'm sure it could be done on a laptop or tablet.

Finally, you'll need some software; I use Serif PagePlus for almost everything, but Photoshop is useful if the perspective of the image has to be corrected before you can use it. I have no connection with any of these firms, by the way.

A simple Inkjet printer is fine for printing off the finished image but for multiple copies take that sheet down to the local print shop, it will be cheaper than doing it yourself, quicker and the photocopier uses spirit based ink which is not affected by damp, sunlight or fading. I print the master copy on gloss photo paper for the best possible image.

So, let's assume you want to model a building with a red brick wall something like this………….

First you need a photograph of a real brick wall, because real photographs are the basis for all these papers which is why they look so realistic. You may want to take the picture yourself, in which case try to get about six to eight square feet of wall in the shot with no shadows or other distractions….something like this:

This is perfect; enough variation in tone but not too much, no shadows and nice and square. Pictures don't usually come out that well, though, but don't worry, they can be manipulated. Upload the image from your camera and open a folder on your computer labelled 'Building papers' or something similar so it's easy to find when you need it.

One picture like that is no use to us for building a model, of course, so it has to be worked on until it fills an A4 sheet. First load the image into PagePlus, keeping it nice and big for the time being. Then right hand click on the image and click on 'copy, then 'paste'. A second image will appear just like the first which can be dragged across until the two are side by side, effectively becoming one image:

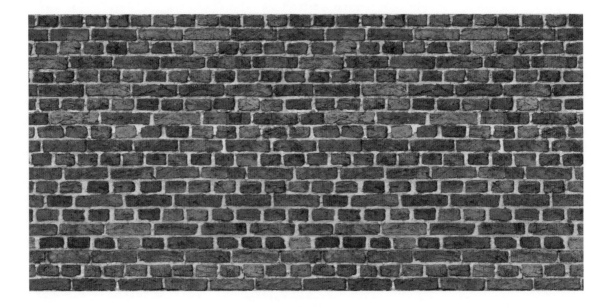

Continue clicking on 'paste' and more copies of the same image will appear, so that you can build up a row of them:

Now is the time to get those bricks just the right size for your scale….don't forget, this sheet can be produced in any scale you like, whether it's 2mm or G Scale. If you are only likely to be needing it for one scale it makes sense to get it the right size now. Resize the image until the bricks look the right size, then print it off and measure one….this is easier and more accurate than trying to do it on the screen. Most bricks should be about 9" long, certainly the factory produced ones used on railway buildings, so 3mm long in 4mm scale is what you are aiming for. You might have to resize it several times until it's right—I always do.

Once you are happy that the image is the correct size, save it so that you can get back to this stage if anything goes wrong afterwards. Label it '4mm scale red brick' or something so that it's clear at once what it is.

Now the whole row of images can be treated as one image and copied and pasted to build up row after row until the screen is full:

There's your first sheet of building paper; it really is that simple. However, in practice of course it isn't usually quite that straightforward, so a bit more work may be required.

That first example used the perfect image as a starting point, but of course perfect images are rarely at hand. The image is likely to need some work before it can be used. Worse, you may not be able to take your own photograph...if you model the Denver & Rio Grande but live in Grimsby you've got a problem!

Fortunately help is at hand. A website called **www.cgtextures.com** contains hundreds of images of surfaces that are ideal for our use. It was developed as a resource for computer games designers who needed to create realistic backdrops, but it's brilliant for modelling as well. Professionals pay an annual fee to be allowed to reproduce the images but for your personal use you can download small numbers to use in your modelling.

Have a browse through it—you'll be amazed.

So, let's use an image that is less than ideal to make a sheet of brick paper.

This is much more typical of the sort of picture you might take yourself, though in fact it comes from cgtextures.com.

Before it can be used the image needs to cropped to get rid of the grass and concrete at the bottom, and the half course of bricks along the top. Fortunately it was taken square on so the perspective shouldn't be a problem.

Load the image into PagePlus, and then it can be cropped like this to get rid of the parts we don't want:

What is left should be useable all being well.

Now copy and past the image so that you have two side by side.

There's a problem; where the two images join the bricks don't line up and some red bricks suddenly become blue. The image on the right needs to be flipped horizontally like this:

Now the two images connect seamlessly and look like one; just what we need.

Now, once it has been correctly sized to the scale you are using the row can be filled up, using the first the original image, then the flipped one, going along in turn.

Then there's another problem; look what happens when the whole row is copied and pasted underneath:

That row of lighter coloured bricks at the top looks wrong now; we're going to get a stripe all along each row as we fill up the sheet. Real brick walls don't look like that.

So, the courses with the lighter colour need to be hidden like this:

The lower row is overlapped over the upper one, and then 'send to back' is pressed so that the part of the lower row we don't want to see is hidden behind the upper row and the wall looks fine. Repeat this over and over until your A4 sheet is full of bricks.

So far so good…. what if the image you want to use wasn't quite taken square on? To adjust this, I resort to Photoshop.

Let's take an extreme example; I need to model the hanging tiles on Horsted Keynes station and this was the best picture I had. I could have driven 150 miles to take a better one, but in fact this did the job after a bit of work.

I loaded the picture into Photoshop, and then cropped the image to concentrate on the part I wanted:

Next, using the 'Transform' section, I used the 'Perspective 'and 'Skew' tools to manipulate the image until the tiles were square on with 90 degree corners…..

That rather odd looking image was saved, and then could be loaded into PagePlus and used just as before.

It looks right on the model because it is right, it's a picture of the real thing and you can't get more accurate than that.

Bricks and tiles are easy because they are regular shapes laid in regular courses. What about something a bit more random?

The most difficult surface to reproduce on a sheet is stone where the courses are not regular, in fact it can simply be impossible. Coarse stone actually doesn't lend itself to this process anyway, but a surprising number of different stone surfaces can be printed, especially in the smaller scales.

The amount of variation in the tone and colour of the stonework on these cottages would be very hard to reproduce by painting.

These stone walls are sufficiently smooth to be modelled using printed paper, but creating the artwork is more of a challenge than it is with brick.

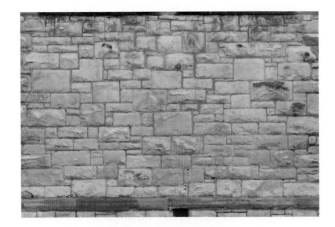

First the image needs to be trimmed to create a useable area.

This is a lot smaller but it is free from the blemishes that would affect the process of repeating it to fill an A4 sheet.

Here the second image has been flipped to reverse it so that the stone courses join up realistically.

Below, the first row begins to take shape.

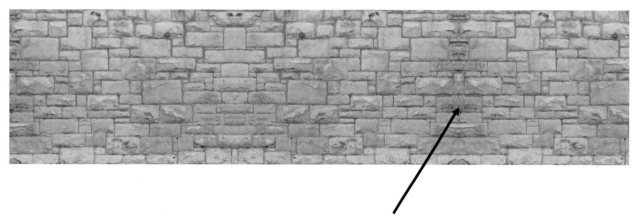

You can see that where the images join there is inevitably a repeating of the pattern which with stone is impossible to avoid; however bear in mind that with a building with openings for doors and windows this won't be noticeable. Large areas such as retaining walls are more of a problem.

I would say that is the ideal place to put a drain pipe!

It is possible to produce very convincing sheets of stone paper, it just needs a little more work in the first instance. Especially in the smaller scales the amount of texture on a stone wall is very slight so a printed paper can look very convincing; being a photographic image the shadows fool the eye into seeing it as three dimensional.

That is the basic technique for producing any printed paper for use on models; it doesn't have to be for a building; sheets of wooden planking are very useful for wagon floors, for instance. Once the original image has been downloaded turning it into a useable sheet of paper for modelling is surprisingly easy and quick.

If you are just producing the sheets for your own use, of course, there is no need necessarily to fill a whole A4 sheet if you don't need to, and slightly ragged edges won't matter. It's what you are going to do with it that is important.

Here's a bit more inspiration!

I defy anyone to paint the brickwork in there!

CHAPTER 4

HOW TO USE THEM.

In this chapter I will concentrate on using printed papers for model buildings as other applications will be covered later in the book, but the techniques are exactly the same whatever the use to which it is being put.

It might seem a little surprising that I need to write a chapter on how to use a sheet of paper, but you'd be amazed how many times I've been asked to explain while doing modelling demonstrations and the like. It's much better to start right from the beginning, and the more experienced can skip that part….we were all beginners once, after all.

Obviously this chapter applies whether you have produced your own papers or are using bought ones, there should be no difference, a sheet of paper is a sheet of paper. However, the grade does vary and in my experience that used in colour photocopiers is generally top stuff which is another good reason not to bother trying to print your own.

TOOLS.

These are basic and simple, but still worth listing. You'll need a scalpel, (much better than a craft knife), and I use Swann Morton 10A blades which are a good multi purpose shape.

A 12" steel rule is also essential for cutting straight lines, and an A3 cutting mat ideally.

None of these are expensive, so when they are worn out chuck them away and get a new one, especially the cutting mat and the blades. A good sharp blade makes a good clean cut, which is what we all want.

A pencil for marking out and a ballpoint pen for scoring folds.

That's pretty much it; you might find items such as a compass cutter useful but for most jobs that's all you'll need.

ADHESIVES.

For nearly everything I use Evostick Imapct glue from a tube; it doesn't smell very nice but it really sticks. You can use other solvent based glue such as Bostick or UHU clear adhesive, but not Copydex or PVA, being water based it crinkles the paper. Stick to a tube glue and you'll be fine.

You do need to keep the glue off the printed surface or it will attack the ink; if you do mess up a piece chuck it in the bin and cut out another, or if it's on the model just stick a new piece over the top. It will happen, sooner or later…………probably sooner!

I am not going to go into detail about constructing the model building, I've written another book which does that. However, I do need to mention that I always construct the shell of the building from plastic card, and complete the walls at least before I put on any papers.

You will have something like this, with the walls assembled and the door and window openings already cut out.

Now it is ready to be clad with the papers.

I cut the papers for each wall flat on the cutting mat before attaching them to the model as far as possible, though sometimes you can stick an oversized piece to the model and trim it in situ using the scalpel if it happens to be easier for that particular application. I do all the marking out in pencil on the back of the paper, though sometimes putting the paper against the model and pricking it with the scalpel blade to mark the size is easier and more accurate than measuring. Anything for an easy life!

When the piece of paper is cut to size, I spread glue over the back of it, in my case Evostick. The instructions on the tube say to spread glue on both surfaces and wait until it goes tacky before bringing them together, but ignore that. Put the glue on straight from the tube; there's no need to cover every patch of paper, in fact too much will just ooze out of the sides and make a mess. All I can say is to try it and you'll soon find out how much is the right amount.

Place the piece of paper onto the model, and you will have time to adjust it so that it is in just the right place. Then use a soft cloth to rub over the surface, which spreads out the glue underneath and makes it all nice and smooth.

I find this is easier than putting the glue on the model, though I'm sure that can work just as well.

That's fine with a plain wall with no openings; what do we do about doors and windows?

Openings are surprisingly easy; you just stick the paper straight over them!

Taking your scalpel, you then cut a vertical line down the centre of the opening from top to bottom, and then along the top and bottom edges horizontally. This creates two rectangular flaps which can be folded back and stuck to the back of the inside wall before the glue goes off. In this way the pattern of the bricks or whatever on the paper is carried around the edge of the door or window which looks better, and the top and bottom edges don't matter because they were often a different material such as a stone window ledge.

Repeat this process for all the openings and suddenly your shell is beginning to look like a building.

Sometimes you'll want to fold the paper around a corner, the easiest way of making the sure the courses all continue at the right level, though if there are stone quoins at the corner this won't be necessary.

Sooner or later you're going to need to join two pieces of paper; if you can, by making each wall a separate piece this can be avoided but on a large building it's inevitable. There are two ways of disguising the joint. The best one is to have it behind a drain pipe! If that isn't possible though, before attaching the paper to the shell take a brown marker pen and draw it along the white edge of the paper; butt join the two pieces on the model and the join will be all but invisible. Don't overlap the papers if you can help it, a butt join looks much better.

On this German station building, although the walls are cream I still used paper for them, simply cream copier paper which did the job perfectly. It was then toned down using weathering powders. This is the same model as in the picture of the plastic shell—what a transformation with a few sheets of paper!

SCORING.

Sometimes it is necessary to fold the paper and to do this neatly it is best to score it on the back before folding it.

For this I use the steel rule and a ball point pen. The pen is ideal, it is smooth enough not to tear the paper yet pointed enough to score it making the fold easy to achieve. A cheap ball point bought in packs of a dozen works for me, as I keep losing them.

Here's why scoring is important:

The ridge tile is a strip of paper scored along the centre line to give a neat, accurate fold. The blue brick at the base of the walls has the top course folded over, which again had to be neat and accurate to make sure they were all the same.

FINISHING OFF.

One disadvantage of printed paper from a photocopier is that it has a slight sheen, so once the model is finished I mask the windows with card held in place with Blutak and spray the whole model with Testor's Dullcote, a matt lacquer which seals everything nicely and gives a dead matt finish. See the last chapter for suppliers of this excellent product, which seemingly like all things that work well smells revolting!

There is one final thing that needs to be done if the model is going to be exposed to damp, perhaps because it is stored in a shed or garage or will be transported to exhibitions in a van.

Paper is affected by damp; it absorbs the moisture and it expands, so bubbles form. They subside again when the paper dries out, but if the paper can be treated to prevent this from happening in the first place then obviously that is a good thing. Fortunately it can, and it's easy to do.

When the whole model is finished, whether it's a building, a platform or whatever, it needs to be painted with a wash of diluted PVA glue, just brushed onto all the paper on the model. The mixture needs to be about as runny as milk, which is what it looks like. This is painted straight onto the paper and allowed to soak in; I use a number 8 brush which seems about the best size unless the area is very large.

The PVA soaks into the paper but it won't affect the printed image; as it dries the paper is stretched flat and when the glue is totally dry the paper is protected from absorbing any damp, as well as being more resistant to scratches, scuffs or other knocks.

This should be done in a warm environment ideally so that the PVA dries fairly quickly, either indoors or in the case of a layout perhaps on a warm day rather than a cold wet one.

This simple technique means that you never again have to worry about the model being damaged by damp, and it is even protected from the weather in the case of exhibition layouts being carried from the van into the hall....a few raindrops won't hurt a model treated with the PVA mixture.

The PVA doesn't need washing up liquid adding to it by the way, as would be the case when fixing ballast; just water is fine.

CHAPTER 5

PAPERS FOR MODEL BUILDINGS

As I have begun by using model buildings as the best introduction to using printed papers it seems sensible to go into a little more detail before moving on to other applications.

If you are still not convinced, have a try at painting some of these, after you've scribed them first of course because no one makes just the right pattern in moulded plastic:

I know two things—my model would be finished first, and it would look better because the finish would be a photograph of a real surface. No contest, is it?

I'd be in the pub while you were still scribing the first wall.

I'll go through some of the commoner building materials and show how realistic a printed image can look.

BRICK. This is certainly the most widely used building material for railway buildings and having a pretty smooth surface is the perfect place to start. There is a lot of variation in the colour of brick, and you also have to consider the pattern of the bonding in which the bricks are laid. There is blue engineering brick, yellow brick, glazed brick, painted brick, the list goes on.

If you are modelling a real building that still survives the best option is to go there and photograph a piece of the real wall, then your paper is going to be perfect reproduction. Usually, though, that isn't possible so all we aim to do is to get somewhere close. The biggest problem is finding a really dirty, smoky wall such as would have been found around a loco shed in the steam age; they simply don't exist any more.

A nice red brick for a fairly dirty environment, ideal for railway buildings. Not only do the bricks vary in tone but the mortar does as well.

Another red brick wall ideal for a situation where things would have been dirty.

A bright orange brick with white mortar, with lots of subtle variation in the colours of the bricks. Ideal for a cleaner situation such as a village street.

This is very different, with an unusual pattern of bonding. The bricks are modern factory produced items so the colour variation on each brick is minimal, but some orange bricks have been used which makes the wall more interesting.

This brick is cleaner and paler, with white mortar so better suited again to a non railway building.

The amount of variation just in those five samples is amazing; there is no such thing as just 'red brick' and slapping on a coat of orange paint is never going to look right. It is the variation in tone, the shadows and the mortar that all add to the overall effect and only a photographic image can really capture that.

Here are some more samples:

Technically red brick, but the overall effect is of a brown wall and the variation in colours is huge, from yellow through red to dark brown. I wouldn't want to try painting that.

This wall uses blue brick and there is still quite a lot of variation in the tone. You might see this on a retaining wall or viaduct.

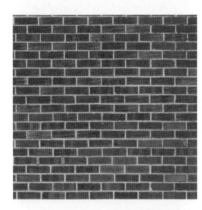

This stretcher bond wall is much less interesting but if you are modelling a modern building this is what you need, with factory produced bricks with little variation.

This fawny yellow brick is old, the bricks are uneven and probably hand made rather than using moulds in a factory. It looks much more interesting, but you wouldn't use it on a station.

A brick wall that has been painted white, as used inside loco sheds and goods sheds to brighten the interior. Look at all those shadows; just painting a piece of moulded plastic white isn't going to achieve that.

The variety is pretty much infinite, so you have to be careful to choose a brick that is appropriate for your building if it is going to be convincing.

Using the correct shade of brick is just as important as painting the woodwork in the correct colour scheme, as is using the correct bond. A GWR Victorian station building such as Culham would look totally wrong if the brick was stretcher bond.

MAKING ARCHED BRICK COURSES. Over many openings in brick walls will be a curved or arched line of brickwork which supports the weight of the wall above it.

This needs to be modelled of course, and happily it's easy to do.

First cut a strip of the brick paper, and then cut along the mortar courses as indicated by the black lines:

The strip will then curve naturally and can then be cut to length and stuck to the wall above the opening; in this case put the glue on the wall and then add the paper strip, not the other way round. These are some examples in place on models:

STONE The other common material for building walls. There is even more variety here, but a lot of stone surfaces can be modelled using printed papers. Some such as Cotswold stone are naturally almost flat, the stone having been sawn into blocks, while others benefit more from the shadows and variation in colour that the image gives.

Quite a rough stone wall with lots of different colours; probably best suited to a background model, but it can look very convincing.

A sandstone wall, actually from Bakewell station; nice and smooth so perfect for our purposes.

A random stone wall with lots of cement between the stones giving a much smoother surface.

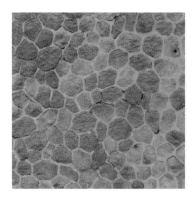

This style of wall is common in France, and the surface is almost flat so it's ideal for printing.

A slate wall with no mortar at all, and with a very flat smooth surface again. Anyone modelling north Wales is going to need a lot of this.

I'm not going to go on with sample after sample, the point has been made. Stone walls can be modelled very convincingly using printed papers.

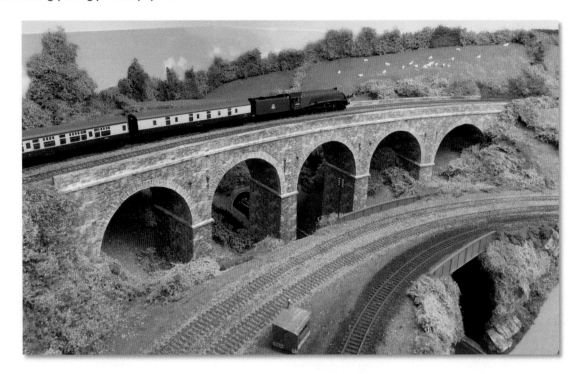

ROOFING MATERIALS The most visible part of any model building is the roof, and here printed papers are really useful as large areas often have to be covered. For years people have been cutting strips pf plastic or paper slates and sticking them on one overlapping the other, tediously working their way up the roof, or even worse sticking on each slate separately.

I'm sorry—not only is life too short, but the end result is usually not convincing. The strips lift and look awful, and the roof still has to be painted. It's not worth it.

This is the way to model a roof:

This is Ashburton station in 7mm scale; look at the amount of variation in the colours of the slates, and then think how long it would take to paint a roof like that.

This is printed paper glued on; it's dead flat, but it looks right because the shadows fool the eye into seeing texture.

Let's have a look at some samples…..

Red clay tiles, which can be seen on a roof or as a wall hanging, usually to keep out damp.

Wooden roofing shingles with moss, not common in the UK but seen all over the US and Europe and very difficult to model to look like this.

The classic slate roof—just look at the different colours and shapes, the chipped edges, the shadows. Slates cut from plastic or card are just too regular.

A slate roof covered with moss and lichen—a real modelling challenge!

Zinc roofing sheets, as seen perhaps as the covering on a station canopy. Just painting the whole lot grey just wouldn't do the job.

I won't go on, you get the picture. Using printed papers is cheap, quick, easy and gives fantastic results.

Buildings are more complicated than that, though. There might be a mixture of brick and stone, for instance:

Here the brick walls were stuck to the building shell first, and then the stone was added on top a piece at a time, scored where it needed to fold into the openings, along the top of the plinth and around the corners. Cutting each piece to fit is simple and doesn't take long, and if one goes wrong just throw it away and try again. Even the platform surface is printed paper here, in Gauge 1. About the only painted plastic you can see in the picture is the door and the window.

The grey stone has that subtle variation and it looks like stone because that's what it is, a picture of real stone.

For this sort of use I prepared myself a sheet of stone strips like this:

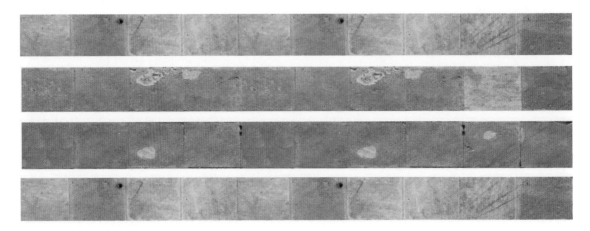

Ridge tiles look similar:

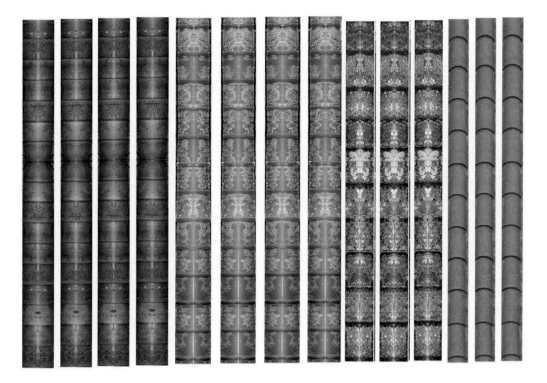

You just cut out the strip, score it along the centre and stick it to the roof, neatly covering the gap where the two pieces of the roof didn't quite meet!

The rounded one on the right is pressed around a length of plastic tube or rod to shape it and then stuck in place; it's strong enough then to stay in shape.

Using ridge tiles in a contrasting colour can be effective:

WOODEN SURFACES. The other really common building material is wood, and again printed papers are very useful.

If a wooden surface is very clean and newly painted I tend to paint it myself as that is replicating how the real thing looked. As soon as there is some weathering, though, or for bare wooden surfaces, printing is the answer.

Some more samples……………..

Even this well maintained painted planking is beginning to show the effects of the weather.

Wood as weathered as this, with just a few flakes of green paint still hanging on, would be very difficult to model any other way.

After a few years of exposure you get this effect, and the printed paper is the ideal way to replicate it.

Unpainted wood is even better with each plank slightly different from the ones on either side.

This is ideal for wooden platforms, the floors of open wagons, there are all sorts of uses.

The commonest colour on railway buildings is cream, and even when well looked after the grain shows through and knots and splits can be seen. Unless it is brand new, just a coat of cream paint isn't good enough.

HOW TO MAKE STAIRS.

A flight of steps or stairs can be one of the hardest things to model as they have to be even, level and straight, with all the steps the same size.

With paper, it's easy.

Cut a rectangle of printed paper the colour of your steps, and on the back draw lines spaced at the size of the steps you want. Draw the lines with a ball point pen so that they are scoring the surface of the paper.

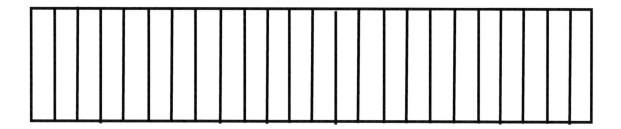

Now fold the paper, first one way and then the other along the score lines to create a zig-zag pattern. Turn it over so that the printed surface is on the top, and you have a flight of steps ready to be used on your footbridge or whatever.

OTHER SURFACES.

To finish this chapter here are a few more ideas for buildings that lend themselves to being printed on paper:

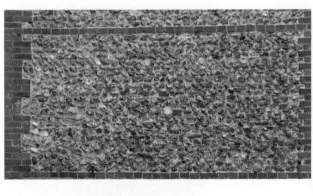  

 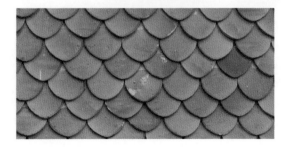

These two pictures show what can be done when time is short and your layout is due at it's first exhibition!

Not only are the walls on the house printed paper, but so are the doors and windows. The carved stone above the archway is flat paper too, and so far not one person has commented on it.

It's all about fooling the eye!

That nice shop window, with the shop interior behind it, is a flat piece of paper with plastic glazing bars stuck on top....the door is paper too.

This is in 1/32nd scale, so its big...just think what you could get away with in 4mm!

CHAPTER 6

PRINTED PAPERS AS SCENERY

For this chapter, I am interpreting scenery as anything on a model railway that is not a building, track or rolling stock. This is a fairly typical scene on a layout.....

It's GCR station in 4mm scale, still under construction when the picture was taken. There is more paper here than you might think...the platform surface, the granite setts leading into the goods yard, the cinder surface in the goods yard, the road over the bridge, as well as the bridge itself and the backscene.

I'm not suggesting that printed paper can take the place of grass and trees, but it has it's place and there are more places where it can be used than you might imagine. As before, it speeds up construction, doesn't make any mess, doesn't need painting and is finished as soon as it's stuck down. There are limitations too, though; look at the curved road leading into the goods yard above. It had to be done in segments, as obviously the paper cannot be curved. To be fair, the same would apply if moulded plastic setts had been used, and I certainly wasn't going to lay them one at a time!

PLATFORMS AND PAVEMENTS Nearly every model railway is going to need a platform, and it's a big area to cover. It has to look convincing because in many ways it's the focal point of the whole layout.

Platforms could be surfaced with stone blocks, brick paving, cinders, asphalt, wooden planks or gravel. I model all these with printed paper. Here are some of the pictures I make use of….

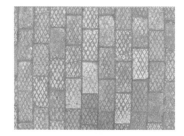

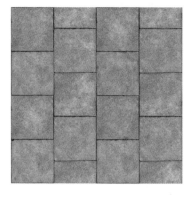

These strips are the platform edging stones, with the white line printed on to save doing it afterwards with paint.

OTHER PAVEMENT SURFACES.

More ornamental surfaces can also be produced, as with these examples:

  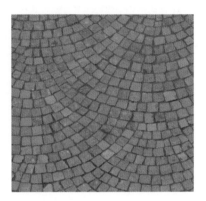

ROADS   All layouts are going to need a road or two of one sort or another. Papers have their limitations because roads tend not to be straight, certainly outside towns and cities, but with care they can still be a valuable modelling tool:

This road on a 4mm scale layout is all paper, and the subtle variations in the colour would be very difficult to reproduce with paint. People tend to model roads so that they are much too dark; because this road is modelled using a photograph of a real surface it is the right colour, a very light grey indeed. Glue was run along the edges of the paper from the tube and static grass strands sprinkled on to cover the exposed edges. Don't use an expensive applicator, by the way, you fingers work just as well!

Modelling a straight road is easy, as these examples show. I have to admit that some ingenuity is required for junctions, though.

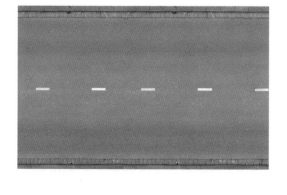
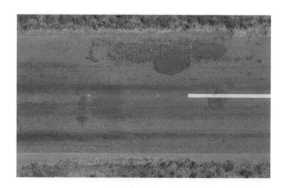

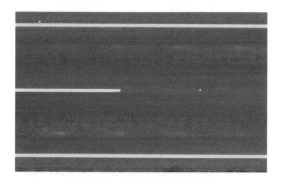

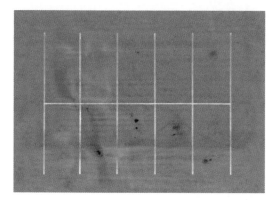

The car park is very useful.

In some ways it is better to use plain asphalt paper with no white lines, and then add those afterwards using paint or paper strips.

Of course not all roads have a tarmac surface, and particularly if you are modelling a layout set before 1939 there should be a lot of granite setts and unsurfaced roads. Goods yards were often surfaced with setts to give a good surface for horse drawn carts, and station approach roads often has these as well....they were later simply covered with asphalt.

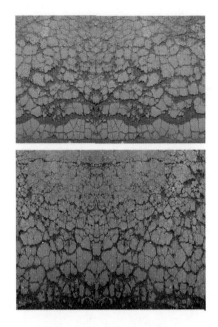

Tarmac weathers in very unusual patterns which show up especially after recent rain as it dries out; I wouldn't want to try reproducing this using paint.

Granite setts soon become overgrown with grass and moss growing in the cracks between them, another feature that would be very difficult to model.

Obviously the grass should have some texture, but I am prepared to overlook that for the realistic overall effect.

Concrete is another surface commonly seen for roads etc. and again simply a coat of paint can't do justice to the many tones present in the real thing. It is just as useful for walls and buildings, of course.

Paper is equally useful for modelling granite setts that are not overgrown, including those laid in fancy patterns. Just look how many shades of grey there are in this small sample.

You can't just stick down a length of grey paper and call it a road; look at any road, particularly in a town, and there will be repairs, inspection covers, drains and the like making it look much more interesting for the modeller.

None of these are difficult to model, and road repairs are very useful if the join between two pieces of paper isn't quite as good as it should have been. I use a strip of paper in a different shade of grey glued over the join and it simply looks as though a trench has been filled in and the surface repaired, realistic and a very useful dodge for covering up gaps.

You can photograph drains and the like yourself, or use the images from www.cgtextures com....here are a few examples:

Just cut them out, draw around the white edge with a brown or black felt pen, and glue them in place. They look remarkably effective.

WALLS Not the walls of buildings, but the walls you might see at the lineside, separating fields or acting as retaining wall.

Here are some samples (and a fence)…..

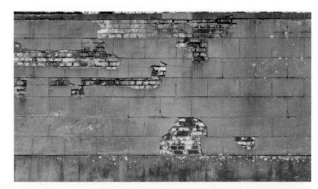

None of these surfaces would be easy to reproduce using paint, and all have a sufficiently smooth surface for them to be perfectly useable printed on paper, even the drystone wall if it is used as a background feature.

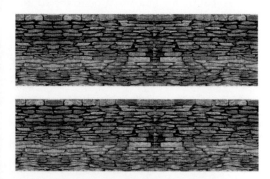

Paper scenery! The road surface is paper, so is the pavement, the picture of the street seen through the arch, the factory building on the left, the road bridge, the factory backscene on the right, and the Lubeck building is clad in paper.

There wasn't room for much scenery, so all the buildings and retaining walls along the back are flat and covered with printed papers, including the windows. The concrete trunking covering the point rodding is covered in paper, too!

CHAPTER 7

LOCO'S AND ROLLING STOCK.

I know what you're thinking—surely you can't have a use for printed papers in modelling loco's and rolling stock?

Well, it's limited, but where I do use it, it's very effective.

Let's deal with loco's first; there is just one place I use paper for on a loco, and it only applies to steam engines. The footplate was invariably wooden planks to give a safe non slip surface for the crew to work on. I model that using paper printed with planks, just cut to fit and stuck in place—easy!

There is a bit more potential with rolling stock.

Open wagons are the obvious place to begin, because the floor of an unloaded wagon lends itself to being modelled with paper, again just a rectangle stuck in place printed with the planks which always ran across the wagon. The wagons sides are more difficult because of the strapping.

So far, pretty obvious. Here's an idea you may not have thought of, though. Vans usually had a planked roof covered with canvas, to keep the weather out. Certainly in the larger scales, 0 Gauge and above, it's worth doing this properly with a sheet of paper printed with an image of real canvas.....you can actually see the weave.

On a really old wagon, you can even model the torn edges.

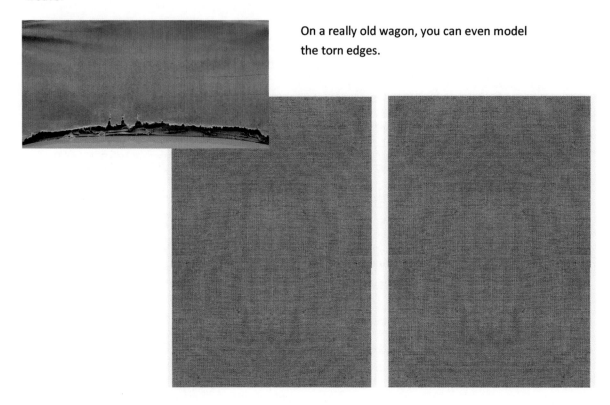

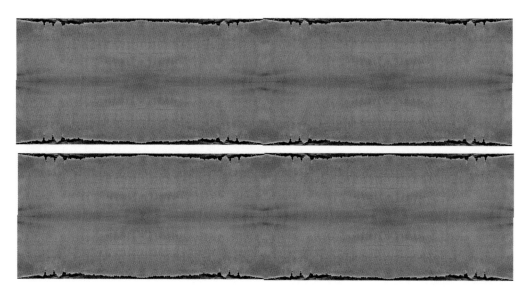

These worn canvas roofs look surprisingly effective as long as it's only done on one or two wagons....not many would have been allowed to get into this condition.

CHAPTER 8

SIGNS, NOTICES AND POSTERS

Small details such as these bring life to a scene and all are easy to produce for yourself, or can be bought ready to use if you prefer.

ENAMEL ADVERTS. The steam age railway was plastered with enamel metal advertising signs, as was much of the adjoining town. They were virtually indestructible and many survive today on preserved lines where of course they can be photographed.

This sort of photograph is ideal, taken at Horsted Keynes station:

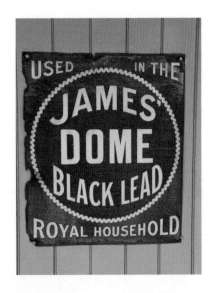

Cropping the image gives a nice square sign ready to use on the layout once it has been reduced to the correct size. A new sign can be printed on gloss photo paper to give that shiny surface, but signs that had been out on all weathers for a long time soon lost any shine.

You can't really have too many of these signs, they were everywhere, which is a good thing because they're fun to make.

RAILWAY POSTERS AND POSTER BOARDS. Another feature of every station up to the present day is the poster board, which came into use around the 1890's when colour printing of posters became cheap enough for mass production. Each railway company has their own design, but they were all basically the same and dictated by the standard size of the posters. A wooden board had a beading around the edge, and a horizontal piece across the top splitting it into two sections, the lower carrying the poster and the upper the company name or initials. These could be painted, fixed using cast iron letters, or using an enamelled plate.

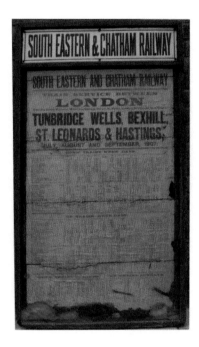

This unrestored SECR poster board is typical, with the full company name on a small rectangle of enamelled metal at the top. Many railways simply used their initials, as in 'GWR' or whatever.

Colour schemes varied, though black with white lettering was common.

My book 'Station Colours' gives full details of the colour schemes used by all the main railways.

Modelling poster boards is easy using PagePlus again; start off with a simple rectangle. Draw the board much larger than the size you want to begin with and then reduce it to size when it's finished.

To source the posters, you can take photographs of examples at preserved lines, or simply Google 'GWR posters' or whatever and up will come lots of pictures. If you are just doing this for your own use there is no problem over simply downloading the images and making use of them.

I back the paper poster boards with a piece of thin black card to beef them up a bit, cut them out and stick them to the wall—job done.

Other station signs such as 'WAY OUT' or 'GENTLEMEN' can be done is just the same way.

OTHER ADVERTISING. In the 20th Century large adverts pasted to hoardings became common, and are easily made, again sourcing the adverts from the internet.

Line side hoardings are easily made from plastic card with Plastruct strip for the support timbers if they are free standing, but it is important to make sure that the posters are correct for the year in which your layout is set. Posters change pretty frequently so you wouldn't have one advertising a film released in 1975 on a layout set in 1980.

Fortunately for most periods images are fairly easy to locate though it gets more difficult as you go back in time. For any urban layout set after about 1900 some hoardings can be justified:

They didn't exactly enhance the environment, but they certainly add colour to a layout.

SLOGANS PAINTED ON WALLS. Another common sight in large towns was an advertising slogan painted directly onto a wall, often an end of terrace facing the railway line. This can again be reproduced using PagePlus:

First open the artwork for the building paper you want to use to model the building.

Onto the image of the bricks write the lettering for the slogan, and drag it to enlarge it to the correct size and shape.

I like the bottom one, where the white lettering has been faded to allow the brickwork to show through, as though the lettering has been on the wall for many years.

Now you just print off your new sheet of brick paper and use it on the model like any other.

This is how it looks in practice, much more interesting than just a blank wall.

You can also use other backgrounds for printed lettering, such as wood which can look very effective for signs, shop fronts and the like, such as this American example. .

Here are just a few examples of the sort of thing that can be achieved by using a background picture of real wood and then applying the lettering over it. The faded signs can look really effective.

This is the perfect way of reproducing a sign such as this one if it isn't possible to use the one from the original picture. Maybe you want to use a different name, or a different colour scheme....it's easy.

PagePlus has a huge number of different fonts including some that replicate a hand painted sign such as this one.

Not a sign or a notice, but here's another tip you might like to have a play around with, particularly if you're modelling an American scene in a fruit growing area. There are lots of pictures on the internet of the labels used on fruit boxes; my layout is set in California so they're perfect. They're colourful and distinctive:

They are no use as they are, though; on a layout we need the actual boxes. With a little playing around on PagePlus, here's the result, ready to be cut out and glued together. Obviously you can print of as many as you want.

They look great by the open door of a boxcar, or piled on the loading dock ready to be shipped. Don't think this only applies to US layouts, though; the technique is the same for any kind of box.

CHAPTER 9

INTERIORS.

Sometimes it's nice to model a full interior in a building, but as it is only going to be seen through a fairly small window there's no point spending too long on it.

You will not be surprised to learn that printed papers are useful here too!

I go into detail about modelling interiors in my book on scratchbuilt buildings, so here I'll just concentrate on the role printed papers have to play. There are two main areas in an interior, the wall and floor coverings and the furniture.

This is the sort of thing to aim for:

Other than the furniture, almost everything you can see here inside the rooms is printed on paper. Using paint inside buildings is risky with those nice clear windows that can no longer be replaced, so using paper is sensible.

FLOOR COVERINGS. The type of floor covering you might want depends on the building you are modelling; a station might have bare boards, lino, tiles or paving while a domestic building may well be carpeted.

Let's start with carpets. Fortunately in the scales we are using the pile of a carpet is so fine that it can safely be ignored, even up to 16mm scale and G Scale. They use real carpet in 1/12th scale dolls houses, but we can forget about that.

The best source of images is to look on the internet at the websites of carpet manufacturers, who use pictures of their products that we can download and use. These are likely to be too small for our purposes so they need to be loaded into PagePlus and enlarged in the same way as the brick paper, by copying and pasting. Here are some examples I have used….

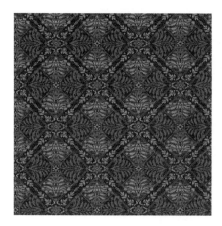  

Once printed and stuck to the floor of the room they look really convincing as the picture on the previous page shows.

Planked floors can use some of the wooden planking we have already looked at, though polished wooden floors might need to be done specially using the same method as for the carpets:

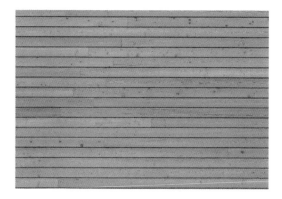

Lino is basically just a brown surface with little variation, while paved and tiled floors can use images from the internet in the same way as shown above. Bathrooms and kitchens especially might well make use of these.

Whatever sort of floor you want, you'll find an image you can use.

Some rugs might be useful...........

WALL COVERINGS For plain walls just use coloured copier paper in pastel tones, maybe cream or light green, the commonest colours for stations when interior walls were distempered. For domestic buildings though you can be a bit more adventurous, with some nice wallpaper, sourced from the websites of the manufactures or retailers. Those that specialise in retro styles are especially useful. They only tend to give a small sample so some copying and pasting will certainly be required here, but the results can be very satisfying.

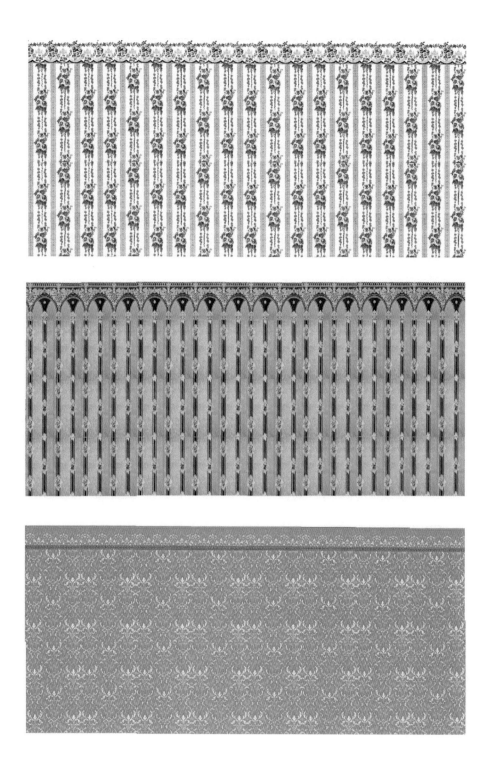

I can't think of another way of reproducing surfaces such as these. A strip of white plastic finishes things off with the skirting board.

Once the floors and walls are covered the real fun begins!

The only limit is your imagination; other than the furniture it can all be done with printed paper.

If you are detailing an interior make sure the roof can be removed in case something comes loose. A simpler alternative is to simply suggest that there is an interior as with this cottage....just an open door and a little wallpaper and you think the whole hall is there behind the door.

Even if you are not modelling the full interior you can suggest it's there; on a house you should certainly add the curtains behind the windows, with perhaps a net curtain as well at ground level. A window sill with a vase of flowers or a sleeping cat, and it looks as though the whole room is there just out of sight. You're tricking the eye again.

The curtains on these cottages are just simple strips of coloured paper, but they make all the difference to the look of the windows. In the upper picture the doors and the stone path are paper too.

CHAPTER 10

BUILDINGS FROM PHOTOGRAPHS.

This is a totally different technique but as it uses printed paper as the basis for they model it is appropriate to devote a chapter to it.

I was faced with building a model of this in HO scale for John Smith's layout 'Torcy'. It is the Mairie at Torcy le Grand in Normandy and the layout wouldn't be Torcy without it.

It took me quite a while before I worked out how to do it.

It's a lovely building, but look at all that decorative brickwork...and in HO too!

In the end I tumbled how to set about it...I used the photographs and made myself a kit. Here's the finished model....

I know you won't want to make a model of this building, but in the smaller scales the technique could be used for a lot of different prototypes. I uploaded the photo on the previous page into PagePlus and did this to it…..

First I adjusted the perspective using Photoshop, then cropped the image to just the part I wanted to use.

I ended up with this; looking good, but the flowers were blocking the door.

A bit more cut and paste and this image was the basis for the front wall of the model; it just needs resizing now to the correct scale and cutting out.

I don't think I could have reproduced that brickwork by trying to paint it.

The ends were done in the same way, and then the rear wall by using the first image but covering the door with a third window by copy and paste.

The four walls were printed twice, the windows and door cut out of the first one and then that was stuck over the second to give a little depth to the openings, as well as thickening and strengthening the wall.

The four walls were glued to a plastic card shell, and the arched lower part was built up in plastic card. The roof structure was plastic, covered with paper slate sheet and grey ridge tiles. The steps up to the door were made up from plastic and painted and that was about it. The printed Geraniums were covered with plastic strip window boxes and flowers from Mininatur.

The chimneys are a length of plastic square rod covered in spare paper from the front wall.

Then John said he wanted the Café too!

This was modelled in exactly the same way.

It's not an exact replica, but it should be recognisable.

CHAPTER 11

SMALL SCALE MODELLING.

By small scale I really mean 2mm scale, and when I was asked to make the buildings from St Ives in that scale I adapted the techniques described in the last chapter to create the models.

I had all the information I needed because I have built St Ives in Gauge 3, 0 Gauge and 4mm scale so I was pretty familiar with it already. What I had never done was work in 2mm scale.

This is what I did:

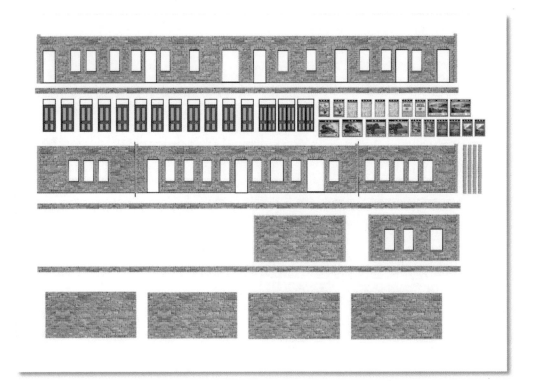

Using PagePlus I drew myself a paper kit. This is the station building. There are the walls, the doors, poster boards and other lengths of stone for overlays, and if I was doing it again I'd include the windows as well. Then it was simply a case of cutting it out and assembling it, knowing that if I made a mess of things I could soon print off another and start again.

I did similar kits for the goods shed and the loco shed.

Both include the whitewashed stone interior walls.

These are the finished models; I enjoyed the experience but I'm not sure I'd want to do it again, I'm happier with things I can see!

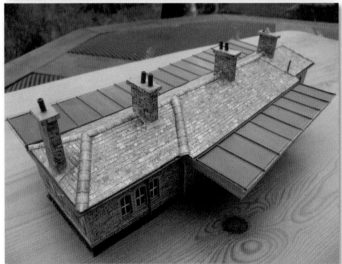

Yes, you can read the nameboard!

CHAPTER 12

LARGE SCALE MODELLING

Having gone to one extreme with 2mm scale, let's head in the opposite direction with some really big stuff, G Scale and 16mm scale. Surely you can't use printed papers in this size, can you?

Have a look at this picture:

This pair of houses were built for a 16mm scale narrow gauge layout, and they were big!

The roof on each is vac formed plastic, the flint walls are budgie grit, but…..all the bricks are printed on paper.

They look OK, don't they?

Printed paper still has plenty of uses in large scale modelling, you just have to use it a bit differently and know when it's appropriate. Even in this size I don't think I could have painted the bricks to look as realistic as this, and frankly I wouldn't bother trying. Those curtains are paper too.

This house was also 16mm scale—I could hardly lift it ! Again the walls are covered in grit, but the stone you can see is all printed paper. The variation in tone is crucial to the realistic look of the model in my opinion. The mullioned windows were easy to model using paper over the plastic frames, and I think they look convincing. The house had a full interior, so there was lots of wallpaper and so on in there.

In any scale, it's seeing where it is advantageous to use something and where it is not, whatever the material or technique may be.

Below is a 16mm scale gatehouse with more printed brick.

Printed papers for the bricks and the woodwork on this charming little convenience. It's 16mm scale again, and the doors open so that you can read the newspaper...and in this scale the Kent Advertiser heading is perfectly legible!

Ebay is a fantastic source of old magazines & newspapers; just put in '1935 magazine' or whatever, and up come lots of pictures for you to download. Maybe better suited to this scale than 2mm!

This is St Ives in Gauge 3 (the same scale as G Scale), and yes, you can read the covers of all the magazines on the book stall!

CHAPTER 13

BACKSCENES

This chapter is not about creating a backscene, but adapting one to make it your own.

To me, a backscene is a crucial part of any layout, but a badly done backscene can ruin everything. Very few people can paint a convincing backscene themselves, so my advice is don't try, do it this way instead. This is why you need a backscene:

Without the sky behind the train this scene wouldn't look convincingly realistic; it's essential to have a backscene, for photographs and simply for viewing the layout. It tricks the viewer into thinking the scene carries on into the distance rather than just stopping at the wall of the room.

This is a commercially produced backscene, as all I wanted was sky...the rest is three dimensional model. However, there are times when that won't be enough and we can do some work to personalise things, particularly by adding buildings. By producing these yourself you will create a scene that no one else has, and you can set the layout in a particular region and time period much more convincingly than any commercially produced backscene can do, as they are naturally trying to appeal to the widest possible market.

This is the sort of thing you can achieve.

This scene is only 15" deep, and finishes where the low stone wall is. However, because of the backscene the eye is drawn into the scene, to the house and beyond it; the scene looks deep. The basic backscene is a Gaugemaster product, a bland scene of countryside and sky, perfect for this situation.

The house, though, I added myself. It is supposed to be a narrow gauge line in Picardy, so I simply Googled 'Maison Picardie image' and up came lots of lovely pictures. I uploaded this one into PagePlus, resized it and printed it off. I cut out the image, drew around the exposed white edges with the brown marker pen, and glued it to the backscene. Some Woodland Scenics foliage finished the job off.

Without the house, the picture would be less effective, and it wouldn't look like Picardy. By adapting the commercial product to suit my needs I have made it personal, individual and much more convincing.

You can do the same.

Berkeley Road in 4mm scale.

Let's have a look at some more examples.

This is John Smith's HO layout Torcy; the station building is on the left. The house is a flat picture on the backscene, as are the hills behind it, but you'd swear that you were looking into the distance. In this case the house is actually from Torcy, John took the photo himself which is even more satisfying.

A backscene doesn't have to be beautiful blue sky and rolling hills of course; here the retaining wall and everything above it are flat backscene, but it really gives depth to the scene. Overlapping the pictures of the buildings gives the impression that some are further away.

Here's another trick, the three dimensional backscene; this is Bodmin Gaol on Peter Clifton's model on Bodmin North. It's 7mm scale and it's huge, but it does a great job of disguising the corner of the room. There's no reason why flat images and three dimensional models shouldn't be mixed to create the scene you want.

In this picture, the chapel is a flat picture on the backscene but the buildings either side of it are low relief models so it looks as though you could walk up the steps and into the scene.

On my 0n30 layout 'Grass Valley' the backscene is barely noticed, but that house makes you think there is more beyond rather than just a sheet of plywood and some paper. Really the backscene is doing its job if you don't notice it, you shouldn't be distracted by it from looking at the actual models.

When the picture on the backscene is doing its job it's amazing how convincing it can be— it really looks as though the road runs through the arch and on into the distance, but in fact both road and arch are a flat picture. It took me a long time to find the right one, but as soon as I saw it I knew it would be perfect for the situation.

There is a lot more you can do with a backscene than just adding a few cut out buildings to the scene, though. Suppose you want to create a whole building to be part of the scene?

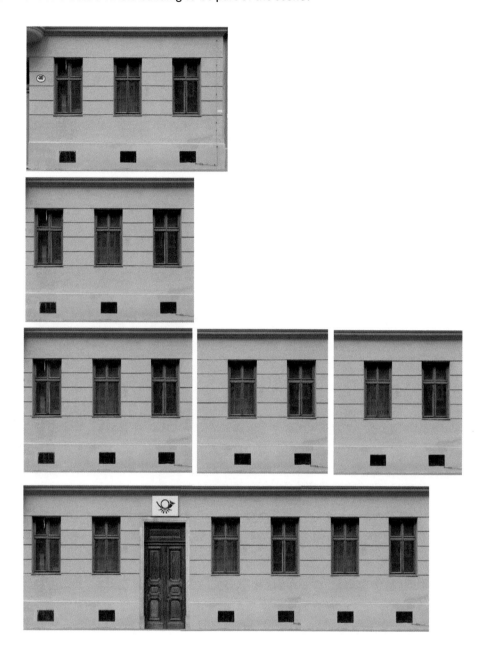

This German post office building began with the top picture, taken from www.cgtextures.com. The image was loaded into PagePlus and cropped to get rid of the shadows at each side, then it was copied and pasted. The new image was reduced in length, again to get rid of a shadow, then copied once more. With the three pieces joined together a door was added, also taken from www.cgtextures,com, and finally the logo of the German post office….all ready to be printed, cut out and added to the backscene. The top edge will close to the top of the backscene on the layout—perfect for filling that gap to the right of the station building.

Suppose you've got a long run of backscene on an urban layout; perhaps a factory building might fill the gap nicely.

I began with a picture from www.cgtextures.com which was simply copied and pasted, then joined to make a longer section of wall. In the lower picture, a section with a door has been added to vary things a little.

The building if fairly nondescript, just what you want on a backscene.

Let's be more adventurous.

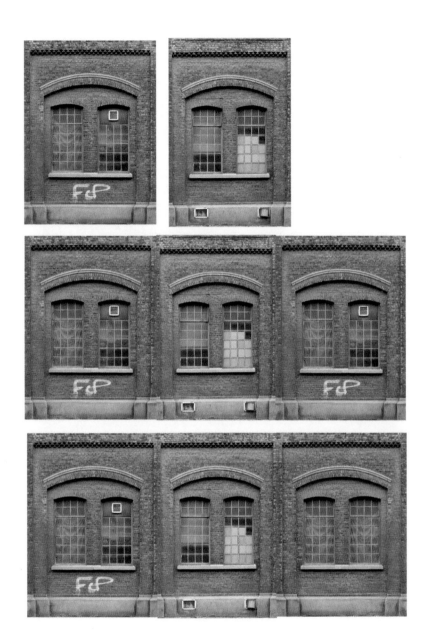

Here two pictures of a factory wall have been used, to begin with simply copying and pasting them, then joining them to make a longer building. There's a problem, though, because every time the image is copied you get the graffiti repeated, and the distinctive windows. In the bottom picture the graffiti on the right has been covered with a section of brick taken from the middle picture, and the windows have been altered simply by copying an image, cropping around the window you want to use and then pasting that over the window you want to cover up.

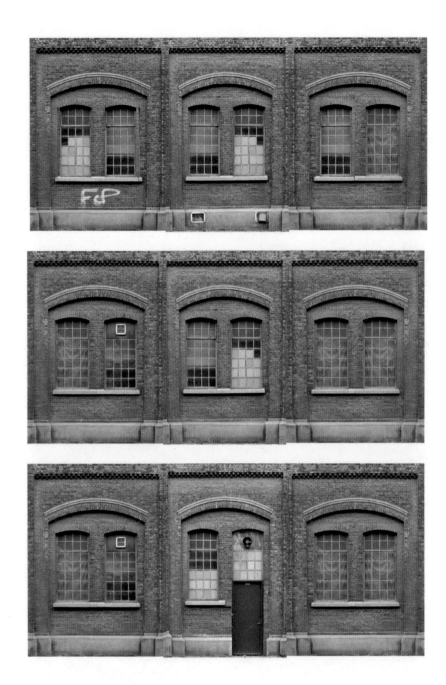

Here things have been developed even more; in the top image the windows on the left are a copy of the ones in the centre, but the image has been flipped so they look different.

In the centre, the two metal ducts have been covered up using a section of stone from the other picture, and the windows are different again; the graffiti has disappeared too.

Finally at the bottom a section of wall with a door has been included; it isn't a perfect match, but backscenes aren't studied closely, it's the overall effect that matters. Working like this a long section of factory wall can be produced without any of the pictures used being exactly the same, and it can look very realistic indeed.

This is the sort of scene you can create; the factory on the backscene is totally flat and everything on it is printed, including the windows.

Below is the post office building from the first example in place on a layout still under construction.

CHAPTER 14

GALLERY

To finish off, some more pictures with notes about how the printed papers were used and the advantages of using them.

These two pictures illustrate another technique, where a building has the name painted on the wall...it's similar to the painted advertising, of course. Being able to curve the roof over those roof lights was useful too.

The swing bridge over the canal at Sharpness, modelled in 4mm scale. With the curved stonework it was a great advantage using the paper as it could be curved around the under-lying structure very easily.

Also in 4mm scale is this canal scene; apart from the obvious benefit of being able to curve the stone sheet around the underside of the viaduct arch, the canal tunnel portal was also on a gentle curve.

Wurzbach also shows the benefits of being able to print the station name directly onto the paper. The enamelled sign on the front is a photo of the real thing reduced in size, so one bit of the model was really accurate!

Hopefully these pictures also show that it is perfectly possible to weather a model clad in paper.

CHAPTER 15

SUPPLIERS

This final chapter lists products and suppliers that I have used and can recommend; I have no connection with any of the firms listed.

As this is my book let's begin with me! My website is **www.kirtleymodels.com** where you will find building papers, posters and all manner of other printed products which I am happy to produce for you in any scale. The books I have written are also listed and can be purchased from Amazon.

SOFTWARE   SERIF PAGEPLUS and ADOBE PHOTOSHOP

ADHESIVES   EVOSTICK IMPACT, UHU, BOSTICK CLEAR.   Easily available on the high street.

MATT SPRAY FOR FIXING IMAGES   TESTOR'S DULLCOTE   EDM Models York www.ngtrains.com

RESOURCE FOR BUILDING PAPERS www.cgtextures.com

BACKSCENES For backscenes printed on self adhesive vinyl.   www.backdropjunction.com

You may also enjoy these books for modellers, available from Amazon or from my stand at exhibitions:

SCRATCHBUILT BUILDINGS THE KIRTLEY WAY

MODELLING SCENERY THE KIRTLEY WAY

STATION COLOURS

Full details of all of them are on **www.kirtleymodels.com**

Printed in Great Britain
by Amazon.co.uk, Ltd.,
Marston Gate.